Anxiety in Relationships

How to Stop Feeling Insecure and Worrying in a Relationship

Rebecca Solis

Table of Contents

Introduction

A nxiety is a part of all life activities; it is also a universal and emotional feeling. Its natural function is to alert us of possible threats so that we can assess them accurately and respond to them effectively. This increased preparation can also enable people to boost their efficiency and enhance innovative drives. Anxiety is also seen as a contemporary societal phenomenon and is reflected more and more in the arts, music, literature, and social media. Anxiety induces excessive or exaggerated reactions to potential risks, leading to chronic and debilitating symptoms related to anxiety disorganizations like fear, phobia, and repetitive behaviors, which also undermine other people's lives.

Anxiety is a normal human condition and a necessary part of our lives. We all have a trait of anxiety in one way or the other. In "fight or flight mode," fear allows us to recognize and respond to hazards. This will inspire us to face tough challenges. The 'right' level of fear will enable us to do more and inspire innovations and practices. Yet anxiety can be viewed from another perspective. Persistent anxiety caused by significant emotional discomfort can lead to unease and, at worst, cause disturbances such as fear, phobia, and obsession. At this point, anxiety may have profoundly distressing and poor effects on our lives and our physical and mental health.

The sense of widespread fear is supported by an investigation commissioned by the Mental Health Foundation. Disturbingly, almost 1 in 5 people have been revealed to have active anxiety "almost every day" or "almost all the time."

The study indicates that 'finance, expenses, and debt' are the most common causes of anxiety and perhaps represents the effect of unemployment and inflation on public health and wellness. Moreover, half of the population has reported that 'people are more depressed than they were five years ago.' Anxiety is among the most widely identified, under-diagnosed, and under-treated conditions within the mental health community. The ability to cope with anxiety is the secret to survival in the face of life. However, knowing it too often means that we risk losing our real self, finding a balance, or relaxing and healing in our lives. We can never be more important to our well-being if we only seek some inner harmony.

This study discusses anxiety as a central component of our nature and part of the natural reaction to human emotions. This is also a challenge to the stigma, which still prevents us from finding support and assistance when our anxiety is becoming a real issue. As individuals and communities, we need to fully understand and participate in anxiety programs, identify the warnings in ourselves and ensure that we have methods to manage it when it tends to harm our emotions. We have to consider if others around us, like friends, relatives, and colleagues, suffer from or are at risk of distressing anxiety due to life events and circumstances. Community public health initiatives have to identify areas of high anxiety and include a continuum of assistance that is non-stigmatic and easy to access. To identify the best places and alliances for those 1 out of 5 people who have problems almost often or always, we urge public health commissioners to look at the list of common online survey sources and use them as a parameter. I believe that public policy will benefit significantly from "fear consciousness" and changing its policies and modes of public interaction to avoid and reduce anxiety. If we honestly understand the rising costs for individuals, their future children, families, and employers with anxiety, we need to act now. This is one of the bases of this book.

It takes a while to stop worrying and keep our anxious thoughts under strict control. Often these thoughts leave us, and we start feeling overwhelmed. Other people have chronic anxiety, leading to daily physical symptoms that are unpleasant or even distressing. These symptoms may grow and cause limiting effects on our lives. Fear can cause these feelings too. Turning to worrisome circumstances can unbalance us, but getting through them can positively affect our lives.

Anxiety will work either for us or against us in an emotional state. It's something that we all share but varies from person to person based on how we experience joy and respond to it. Our lives, education, and personalities all can influence an individual's behavior towards fear during an experience.

Becoming depressed is not a sign of weakness, but anyone under these symptoms needs to see a counselor or a psychiatrist.

Yet, once you begin to better understand anxiety, you can do a lot to reduce the pressure and learn to feel the full spectrum of emotions without thinking about them.

Chapter 1:
What is anxiety and how to recognize it

A nxiety is your mind and body's natural reaction to stressful or dangerous situations. It is a normal response that we all experience at one time or another throughout our lives. However, when an anxiety disorder exists, it can take a heavy toll, both mentally and physically. Anxiety disorders are characterized by excessive fear of real or imagined events that can cause minor or drastic changes in a person's life.

One of the most common symptoms is what's known as an anxiety attack, which a person can experience even when they aren't facing any immediate danger. When something triggers an anxiety attack, the person will usually experience feelings of panic, accompanied by physical symptoms such as sweaty palms, trembling, nausea, elevated heart rate, pain, and difficulty breathing. Anxiety attacks aren't permanent and usually last anywhere from a few minutes to a few hours.

People of all ages can suffer from anxiety disorders, and there are many different causes and triggers for them. For example, the most common reasons for anxiety in children and teens are the pressure to do well in school, bullying from classmates or teachers, sibling rivalry, and upcoming exams. Many young children also face separation anxiety, which happens when the child gets permanently or temporarily separated from one or both parents.

For adults, the causes of anxiety disorders tend to be work-related. Other common reasons for anxiety include traumatic events, the need to meet expectations or fear of failure.

These situations exert immense pressure on the person's psyche, and their fear levels rise as a result. Their mental health suffers, and they begin to do poorly in school or work.

In addition to psychological damage, their physical health will take a hit as well. Stomach problems, erratic heart rate, shortness of breath, nausea, sleeping disorders, and fatigue are all physical manifestations of an anxiety disorder.

There are plenty of things you can do if you or the people close to you display symptoms of an anxiety disorder. Psychotherapy is the best course of action if you see signs of depression or anxiety in yourself or your loved ones. Depending on the severity of the symptoms, a psychiatrist might also prescribe medication. Anti-anxiety medication can provide quick and effective relief from panic attacks, as well as long-term stability. Your psychiatrist will manage the dosage of these treatments and make adjustments as you progress.

Anxiety disorders can further be classified into the following types:

•Generalized Anxiety Disorder (GAD) is a type of anxiety disorder in which a person endures a constant state of stress and depression without any apparent problems or stressors.

People suffering from generalized anxiety disorder find it difficult to sleep and relax their minds. Common symptoms of GAD include shortness of breath, headaches, muscle pain, nausea, trembling, sweating, irritability, and lightheadedness.

•Panic Disorder (PD) is a severe type of anxiety disorder that causes excessive and unexpected terror, which keeps the individual in a state of near-constant fear. This type of anxiety disorder makes the individual unable to make any life decisions. A person with Panic Disorder usually avoids specific situations that can trigger a panic attack. Significant panic disorder symptoms include sweating, trembling, shortness of breath, lightheadedness, GAD, headaches, muscle pain, chest pain, and increased heart rate. People who have Panic Disorder can have a significant fear of sudden death or losing their mental health. Drug abuse, depression, and alcoholism are common problems among people living with PD.

•Agoraphobia is a type of anxiety disorder in which the individual restricts themselves from performing daily activities to the point where they stay indoors for weeks or even months. This is because of their fear, whether real or perceived, of feeling trapped or helpless in a public setting, be it standing in a queue, getting on public transport, or being in a crowd. In this way, they believe they can avoid any situations that can trigger a panic attack.

•Social Anxiety is a type of anxiety disorder that is mostly triggered in social events and gatherings. It stems from the fear of being humiliated or rejected by other people. This makes the individual stay away from parties, dinners, or any social gatherings where the person feels that they will be scrutinized. It is important to note that Social Anxiety is not the same thing as shyness.

Social Anxiety can adversely affect the individual's relationships with their loved ones. It drives a wedge between them and those who love them and want to help them overcome this disorder. That's why it's vital to discuss anxiety symptoms with loved ones. Timely and effective treatment is crucial for people with Social Anxiety to recover their relationships and social life.

•Obsessive-Compulsive Disorder (OCD) is a condition in which the individual becomes unable to control their behavior and actions. Individuals suffering from OCD unintentionally develop certain habits that become part of their routine. Some habits include washing their hands over and over, repeatedly checking or verifying that things are a certain way, and continuously experiencing negative or obtrusive thoughts.

•Post-Traumatic Stress Disorder (PTSD) is caused by a traumatic event in a person's life. A particular memory or flashback associated with the event can trigger a panic attack. People with PTSD display heightened irritability and emotional or physical outbursts when undergoing a panic attack. Drug abuse and depression are common problems of people living with PTSD.

All the above types of anxiety are listed based on their intensity. Anxiety varies from mild to severe and has different effects on each person. As mentioned before, anxiety is an entirely natural behavior that all human beings experience and is sometimes necessary to help identify potential danger. It only becomes dangerous and harmful when it crosses a limit and becomes symptomatic. If you believe that you are experiencing symptoms of anxiety, it is recommended that you seek professional help.

Chapter 2:
How Anxiety Starts in a Relationship

N obody wants to lose their connections with family, friends, and loved ones. Still, the sad thing is that this sometimes happens without us knowing the reasons why. There will always be ups and downs, rude or unkind behaviors, financial problems, work or school pressures, and many other problems in any relationship. We all have different life experiences and go through different mental states throughout the day. Some of these experiences are painful or even traumatic. They can lead to emotional outbursts or unhealthy behaviors that can drive the people around us away. When these behaviors become a regular part of your interactions with your loved ones, they can begin to have a potentially permanent effect on your relationships.

Suppose your partner has never experienced a mental illness. In that case, it can be difficult for them to understand what you're going through.

For example, depression and anxiety often make the person withdraw from social life and their loved ones, which might be very difficult for their significant other to comprehend.

Obsessive thoughts and tendencies are also symptoms of anxiety disorders. It's human nature to want to give and receive love and affection. However, some people can become overly possessive over people and things, which leads to feelings of jealousy and insecurity. When they aren't getting the desired love and attention from their loved ones, they start feeling anxious. They can also experience anxiety or panic attacks when they think they're being avoided or neglected. This is one of the most common causes of anxiety in relationships.

Excessive attachment to a romantic partner is also indicative of an anxiety disorder. Thoughts of separation or not getting the desired attention and responses from their partner can profoundly affect people who suffer from anxiety disorders. A psychotherapist can offer tips to help you be a grounding, supportive presence for your loved one if something triggers an attack. Asking what they need from you and providing love, support, and understanding are crucial when helping a loved one through their symptoms of anxiety and fear. However, keep in mind that severe panic attacks should be immediately reported to their treating specialist.

Self-confidence—or lack thereof—is yet another primary reason for anxiety in a relationship. For many people, anxiety comes from low self-esteem and the belief that they aren't "good enough." As such, meeting new people is often an excruciating ordeal. These feelings of insecurity and inferiority can cause severe stress and depression.

However, you must keep in mind that your low self-esteem is only a product of mental illness. Talk-therapy is a fantastic way to learn to overcome your feelings of insecurity and learn true self-love and acceptance.

Do you ever fear that you aren't "good enough" for your significant other? Or that they "deserve better"? Try talking to your significant other about how you feel. Overcoming these issues can be easier with the right care, support, and attention from family and friends, in addition to therapy and medication. Never take your mental health lightly—opening up to the people who love and care about you is the first step to recovery.

A healthy romantic relationship is one that can roll with the punches, handle the ups and downs, and not be destroyed by the inevitable end of the "honeymoon phase."

Many people entering a new relationship talk about that "butterflies in the stomach" feeling when their new love interest so much as walks by. You have probably experienced it yourself. You want this feeling to last forever and for your relationship to be absolutely perfect. You go out of your way to make the best impression, sometimes at the expense of your true feelings. Maybe you start changing some aspects of yourself to fit with your new partner. You begin second-guessing every decision you make.

At the beginning of a relationship, this level of stress is not healthy and can lead to even more serious problems later on.

Here are some things you can do to overcome the stress of starting a new relationship.

First, you have to identify the root cause of your anxiety and your fears of not being the right person for your partner. When you meet someone you like, you will naturally want to develop a relationship with that person. As you continue with your relationship, you might start thinking negatively about yourself. The bad memories may begin to pop up, re-minding you of things you're not proud of, making you feel unworthy of love.

All these negative thoughts are unreliable, though. More often than not, they come from your anxiety disorder or depression. You have to face them head-on and not let them rule your life—and ruin your relationship.

If you feel ashamed of something in your past, you'll likely experience the fear that your partner will find out about it. While it's important to keep in mind that you are in no way obligated to share every single aspect of your past with your significant other, sometimes keeping a big secret can be very stressful and ultimately harmful to you and your relationship.

Chapter 3:
Insecurity in relationships, how to overcome it, what are the symptoms, and how to recognize them

I seemed to destroy every romantic relationship in which I had ever been involved. Not because of infidelity, nor because of incompatibility. Not even because of fights, boredom, or need for personal space. They were all destroyed because of a trance-like state that would consume my entire being on an extremely regular basis. Almost as if I were possessed by a demonic entity. I would become hyper-vigilant, as observant as a private investigator. I would become a quick and intensely sharp manipulator. Warm anxiety imbrued energy would rapidly swell up from my feet to my stomach, all the way up my throat. I would lose control of my thoughts and words. All of these symptoms were seemingly caused by my obsession with my partner's past. I would bombard my partners with personal questions about their previous relationships. No stone would be left unturned, and the obsessions would fester for days, weeks, months, and years at a time. A myriad of imaginary images and thoughts of my partner's past would be cycling through my mind minute after minute with no respite. When I finally went to sleep, I would suffer an onslaught of nightmares, watching these re-imagined past encounters of my partner play out like a movie. In waking, I would name, blame and call my partner all kinds of derogatory names. I wasn't consciously aware enough to control the outward assault on the world and the people around me.

What Are the Symptoms of Insecurity and How to Recognize Them?

Blaming

If you are always reprimanding or blaming your partner for everything, you need a rude awakening. This happens when your ego is controlling your relationship and utilizing manipulative tactics to do it. Do you ever assume responsibility for the things that you do? Would you be able to take a step back from the situation and think from another perspective without accusing the other person? The ego will want you to find fault and scrutinize for others' mistakes. It will do everything and anything to transfer blame and criticize another person. Shockingly, that thing we evade is generally what we end up receiving in our relationships. If you fail to take responsibility for yourself, your ego will help you project everything onto your partner.

Playing the Victim

Is it safe to say that you are playing the unfortunate victim card in your relationship? Do you always compare yourself with your partner? Is it true that you are continually putting yourself down? An unhealthy ego will help you reinforce negative actions as opposed to positive ones. It will cause you to focus too much on your imperfections. It is unquestionably time to venture back and conduct a recheck on your relationship if you are doing this. You are not a saint.

The time has come to be responsible for what you are bringing to the table and stop constantly blaming your partner for everything.

Being Jealous

Jealousy is the green-eyed monster, and it usually sets the stage for negative drama in a relationship. The ego tends to feed on self-esteem and the absence of acknowledgment. A cherishing relationship depends on the regard and consciousness of each other. Love doesn't contribute to comparing, putting down, and criticizing as ego does. This is a show that turns into the most astounding type of negative drama in any relationship. If you are in an abusive relationship, your ego won't let you leave because of jealousy. What is making you consider these ideas? Does your partner make you question the validity of your relationship? This means you need to venture back and be straightforward about identifying the abuse in the relationship.

Fearing Rejection

This kind of dread prevents you from proceeding onward and accomplishing any of your goals. When you stop yourself as a result of this dread, you are unfair to your relationship. Changing the way you perceive things as opposed to being incapacitated by the anxiety and uneasiness caused by your ego will be a healthy way to increase self-esteem. Negative self-talk will only feed your ego. Don't compromise on who you truly are to surrender to your partner's ego. This is anything but healthy. A loving relationship depends on mutual respect and acknowledgment. On the off chance that you are feeling rejected, maybe it's time to re-evaluate your relationship.

Always Having the Last Word

Your ego has a way of making every little thing about you and turning it into a one-person play. If you find that you talk a lot about yourself and don't ask about your partner, well, you are immensely ego-driven. The ego assumes a superb role in shielding us from accomplishing total harmony and joy. It is the mind's method for controlling. It will likewise create situations in your mind that don't exist. If you find that you need to have the last say in all things, it's time you venture back and discover the root of this need. Do you feel like you are better than others or second rate? Do you lack self-confidence and, in this manner, need to demonstrate that you are worthy despite all the trouble? The ego will make you conceal your sense of mediocrity by overhyping yourself. If you and your partner fight a lot, your ego probably fuels these fights. Is this how you feel important in your relationship?

It is important to take a step back and observe your relationship at times. You need to identify when you are the one in the wrong and making mistakes. Take a look at your actions and acknowledge when they are driven by ego. You have to let go of your ego if you want a strong, healthy relationship with your partner.

So if you have a big ego or your love is egotistical, what should you do?

For the narcissist, being correct all the time is deeply connected with their sense of self-worth. In this way, the individuals who can't relinquish their egos do and say anything they want and always think they are correct. Tragically, this will be at the expense of a lot of other things. Their need to always be correct can cost them their relationship with colleagues, supervisors, relatives, and, more often than not, their partners. Sooner or later, you have to understand that the bogus self-esteem you get from adhering to your ego and "being correct" doesn't exceed genuine happiness.

Being true to yourself and practicing mindfulness will enable you to understand that you can't be right in every circumstance. There will be certain situations where you make a mistake, have a wrong mentality, or are essentially on the wrong side.

It may be hard to admit this at times; however, having the ability to concede when you're wrong can be quite liberating. Assume responsibility for your actions and decisions, and you will soon see that the ball will be in your court!

Understand that you don't have to be better than everybody else either. The need to be this way can be quite destructive for you. A great sense of ego leads you to believe that you are superior to every other person. It is similar to remembering that you don't need to be correct constantly. That is not a healthy level of competitiveness in anyone.

There will always be somebody better, prettier, more astute, quicker, and wealthier than you. No matter how old you are, this will always be the way of things. The sooner you understand that you cannot—and ought not to feel committed to—be superior to other people, the sooner you can repair and improve your relationships.

Rather than contending with others along these lines, why not consider improving yourself? You are perfectly unique. Focus on how you can improve yourself, and every one of your relationships will take a turn for the better.

Exercise: it is imperative to see how activity impacts the body as well as the mind too. Daily exercise is essential in an individual's life. When you exercise regularly, your brain discharges endorphins into your circulatory system, improving your mindset. Besides, your psyche will be occupied for restless musings. Exercising has been deduced to help your general state of mind and decrease the indications of nervousness and sadness. As physical exercise increases, so relieves your anxiety. A few activities to take an interest in that have been explicitly connected to assisting with tension are yoga and judo. This is because these activities help individuals be careful in their development and center themselves spiritually while clearing their brains. As you structure an everyday practice with your activity, your body will start to deliver serotonin and endorphins during and after exercise. These synthetic concoctions that are provided in the brain appear to diminish melancholy and uneasiness fundamentally. Training supports confidence, improves certainty, enables you to start to feel engaged and reliable, and causes you to manufacture substantial and new social connections and companionship.

Begin a healthy diet: the brain requires an enormous measure of vitality and sustenance to work effectively. Healthy nutrition can bring enormous changes in your physical health. A terrible eating regimen implies that you are not providing the required supplements for your brain's synapses to work effectively. In light of that, it might be worsening the manifestations of your nervousness. By following a sound eating regimen and filling your plate with entire and new nourishment, drinking the perfect measure of water, and guaranteeing that you are taking in the correct nutrients, minerals, and Trans Fats day by day, you are giving your cerebrum the proper nourishment to battle anxiety. A solid eating routine likewise implies dealing with your guts and stomach related tract. Recollect that a sound eating routine removes improved beverages like frosted teas, soft drinks, and prepared natural product juices. Studies have demonstrated that individuals who drink an over-the-top measure of pop each day are over 30% bound to experience the ill effects of nervousness and melancholy than those who don't. Unsweetened beverages like plain espresso, home-grown teas, and water that has organic products in it are far more beneficial alternatives when keeping your body and cerebrum hydrated. Caffeine is likewise a supporter of tension side effects and ought to be curtailed to battle caffeine symptoms.

No more liquor: liquor is a focal sensory system depressant and is a known reason for tension, and we all know that it is very harmful to our health. A few people do attempt to dull the impacts of their nervousness by drinking liquor; however, actually, liquor is regularly the base of your tension.

Liquor intrudes on rest, dehydrates the body, and occupies an individual from managing the current issues as opposed to going up against and recognizing the root and reason for their anxiety.

Catch up on your rest: bad dozing propensities affect an individual's state of mind. This is because the brain's synapses need time to rest and recharge to keep the body's mindset steady. Legitimate long rests enable the cerebrum to adjust hormone levels and allow an individual to all the more be likely to adapt to their anxiety. If plagued with unhealthy sleep patterns and sleep deprivation, you needn't bother with synthetic compounds to be amended. Awful resting propensities can be rectified utilizing natural remedies and techniques, including melatonin, teas, homegrown mixes, exercise, and contemplation. When you ensure that you are getting high-quality rest and your mind will start to address its hormone levels.

Begin to address your feelings: this book covers dealing with your negative contemplations and frames of mind broadly. Being restless manipulates the brain into creating more hormonal concoctions to attempt to feel upbeat. In the end, the cerebrum gets exhausted and can't deliver the correct dosage of hormones required to keep your system healthy, happy, and tension-free. Via preparing your psyche to consider re-flection emphatically and care thoroughly, you can change your recognition of what's going on and start to assume responsibility for your negative considerations. By battling and hushing your negative contemplations, you can work through your nervousness, ensuring you are better ready to recuperate in your relationship. Make sure to rehearse all types of positive confirmation, which incorporates excusing yourself, appreciating your life, and showing consideration to other people. When you can get positive, uneasiness begins to slow, and you are better ready to speak with your accomplice without negative, foolish conduct subverting you. Keep in mind that you are responsible for your life. If there are circumstances that are making you tense, you can transform them.

Reduce your pressure: stress builds nervousness higher than anything and triggers the body's battle or flight reaction. By learning techniques to manage pressure and control and focusing on factors, you enable your body to all the more likely deal with its normal reactions to what it sees as a risk. Distinguishing what makes worry for you enables you to either remove the pressure or create methodologies to help you deal with it. Rehearsing unwinding systems, setting aside effort for yourself to revive, and appreciating life are large approaches to loosen up your mind and enable nervousness to ease. Become flexible to stress and realize that, by and by, you have power over pressure.

Reach out and locate a solid help base: a stable relationship begins with solid fellowships. Having a decent informal organization that offers you support and a sounding board as you work through your tension is critical to mending. Uneasiness can make an individual need to detach themselves; however, a decent help structure implies you will consistently have somebody to connect with when tension rears its head. These ought to be individuals who locate the positive things in you and can give you sensible and objective reactions when you talk about what is causing your uneasiness. They should provoke you to investigate inside and should assist you with quieting your inward pundit. Ensure that you keep in constant contact with your loved ones who make you like and love yourself. Do whatever it takes not to become involved with others' pessimism. Attempt to volunteer to increase your perspective in life and associate with others who have emotional wellness issues. On the off chance that you are not yet at the point where you need to see an advisor, attempt to join a care group. Consider adopting and caring for a pet to help soothe your nervousness and show you unconditional love.

Find your motivation: people who have a definite feeling of their motivation can better deal with pressure and nervousness than those who don't. Finding your inspiration gives you a boundary against the impediments your internal pundit outlines for you. Those with a solid feeling of direction will, in general, find life to be all the more satisfying and can see the positive qualities in each circumstance instead of stressing over what terrible events may occur. Your motivation doesn't need to be a vocation or a leisure activity. Finding your otherworldliness, investing energy considering your qualities, volunteering at covers or no benefit associations, recognizing and utilizing your one-of-a-kind gifts to help other people, and recognizing that life is about rhythmic movement are, for the most part, methods for finding your motivation. When you discover your motivation, you can get strong and fair with yourself, enabling you to be straightforward with your accomplice.

Chapter 4:
Self-Evaluation of Anxiety in a Relationship

How do you know you are anxious in a relationship? What are the signs that show that you are having a negative emotion concerning your relationship? What are the effects of anxiety on your relationship? All of these questions will be answered when you carry out what is called a self-evaluation of relationship anxiety. This chapter focuses on the self-evaluation of tension in a relationship. The essence of this is to evaluate the issue to put an end to it.

Anxiety can spring out at any time in a relationship. The fact is that everyone is vulnerable to this problem; the tendency to become anxious in a relationship increases as the bond becomes stronger. So, there is a need for everyone to carry out a self-evaluation.

Do you spend most of your time worrying about things that could go wrong in your relationship? Do you doubt if your partner really loves you? A sure sign of relationship anxiety is when you become worried all the time as a result of these and similar questions running through your mind.

For proper self-evaluation of this problem, you need to know the signs that show that you are already becoming anxious. Also, you need to weigh the cause and effect of this problem on your relationship. As I have said earlier, the purpose of evaluating is to address the issue before it develops. This chapter is structured to give you maximum benefit, and I will try to be as explicit as possible.

How to Know if You Are Getting Anxious in a Relationship

You might be neck-deep in relationship anxiety without really knowing, so this section will point out the symptoms of this problem to you. If you notice any of the signs mentioned below, you will benefit greatly from the self-evaluation process.

When you feel jealous of your partner

Take a cursory look at your behavior. Do you feel like breaking somebody's head when your partner develops any form of a platonic relationship with the opposite sex? Are you threatened by any friends of theirs you fear may "steal" your partner away from you? This is jealousy, and it is one of the signs that you are feeling anxious in your relationship. Sometimes, you might even have the urge to test your spouse's commitment and love; this indicates anxiety triggered by jealousy.

When your self-esteem is low

When you are always cautious of how you behave because you don't know what your partner's reaction will be, or you can't express yourself freely in front of your partner due to fear of rejection, this is an indication of low self-esteem - a sign that you are anxious in your relationship.

Lack of trust

Your partner is one of the people you should trust the most. If you always have to confirm whatever your wife, husband, boyfriend, or girlfriend says before you believe them, it shows a lack of trust in the relationship. Many times, the lack of trust is caused by past betrayal. However, you should not allow past betrayals to negatively impact your relationship, provided they were one time occurrences. Realize that your partner is not perfect, and once they have assured you that such incidences will never happen again, believe them.

Emotional imbalance

Today you are frustrated, tomorrow you are angry; the next day, you are happy – this is emotional instability. You might not be aware of this, but constant mood swings are also signs of emotional imbalance, and they do not help the matter.

They only worsen it. Whatever problems or issues you are facing, discuss them with your partner. When the two of you deliberate on a problem, you will get it solved quickly. When you discover that your mood is not stable, it is a symptom of anxiety in a relationship.

Lack of sleep and reduced sex drive

The aftermath of constant worry is insomnia, which is the inability to sleep, and when you are unable to sleep, your body is stressed, leading to decreased libido.

If you are experiencing one or more of these symptoms, you need to figure out the possible causes and deal with them. I am going to give you examples of likely causes of these problems.

Possible Causes of a Relationship Anxiety

Most times, relationship anxiety could be a manifestation of a deep-rooted problem. Here are the common causes of relationship anxiety:

Complicated Relationship

When you are uncertain about your relationship, or it is not clearly defined, it can be classified as complicated. This applies to those that are dating. For instance, a woman may not know the man's intentions - whether he wants to marry her or is just in it for fun. Also, a long-distance relationship could result in anxiety. In such cases, partners must learn to trust each other.

Comparison

Comparing your current relationship with past ones should be avoided as much as possible. You might begin to entertain feelings of regret if you discover that your previous relationship was better in the areas of finance, communication, sex, and other aspects. To avoid this feeling, you should never compare your marriage or relationship to that of others or those you have had in the past.

Constant fighting

When you are always quarreling with your partner, you might never stop worrying because you don't know when the next altercation will crop up. This is one of the causes of severe anxiety in a relationship because your bid to avoid quarreling will not allow you to have a pleasant time with your partner.

Lack of understanding

Partners that do not take the time to understand each other will always face difficulties. As mentioned earlier, the constant quarreling will result in an anxious relationship. Are you noticing the symptoms of anxiety coupled with miscommunications? Lack of understanding might be the reason for your relationship anxiety. Get to know your partner better, and encourage them to know you.

Other issues

Difficult experiences in past unhealthy relationships might result in many other issues. Not only that, neglect during childhood, abuse in the past, and lack of affection are reasons why someone can feel anxious in a relationship.

Once you have identified the root cause of your relationship issue, getting rid of it will be the next step. Do not forget that the primary reason for the self-evaluation of any problem is getting rid of it.

Effects of Anxiety on Relationships and How to stop it

This section will examine the effect of anxiety on a relationship with logical steps towards ending it and how anxiety manifests in a relationship. The effective ways to stop it, no matter the way it appears, will also be highlighted.

Anxiety makes you continuously worry about your relationship

Persistent worry is one of the manifestations of relationship anxiety. If you are continually having thoughts such as, "Is my partner mad at me?" "Are they pretending to happy with me?" or "Will this relationship last?" These kinds of views indicate one thing – WORRY. If you discover that you regularly entertain these kinds of thought, do the following:

·   Clear your mind and live in the moment.

·   If negatives thoughts are continually running through your mind, then stop, clear your mind, and think about the beautiful moments you have shared with your partner. Think about the promises your partner has made, and reassure yourself that your relationship will stand the test of time.

- Do not react impulsively - think before you take any step. Share your feelings with your partner rather than withdrawing from them - make an effort to connect.

Anxiety breeds mistrust

Anxiety makes you think negatively about your partner. You will find it difficult to believe anything they say. In some cases, you may suspect that your partner is going out with another person. These kinds of feelings inevitably come between you and your partner. It makes it hard for you to relate to them well. To put an end to this, follow these practical steps:

- Ask yourself, "Do I have any proof of my suspicion?"

- Go to your partner and talk things over with them.

- Start again if you notice that your relationship is suffering from a lack of trust.

- Reestablish the trust, date each other as if it is your first time, and gradually build the trust.

- Do the things you did when you first met each other.

Anxiety leads to self-centeredness

What anxiety does is take all your attention, making you focus solely on the problem while every other thing suffers. You don't have time for your partner; you are withdrawn into yourself. You focus mainly on yourself and neglect the physical and emotional needs of your partner. Here are the things to do to get rid of this attitude:

· Rather than magnifying and focusing on your fear, pay attention to your needs.

· You can seek your partner's support when you discover that you cannot handle the fear alone.

Anxiety inhibits expression with your partner

Anything that stops you from expressing your sincere feeling to your partner is an enemy of your relationship. Anxiety is the culprit here; it hinders you from opening your mind to your partner. You think that they might rebuff you or that telling them how you feel may cause an adverse reaction from them. This makes you keep procrastinating instead of discussing the critical issues right away with them. How do you overcome the fear of rejection? Consider the following quick steps:

- Focus on the love your partner has for you.

- Voice out what you feel to get rid of anxiety.

- Approach your partner cheerfully.

- Discuss heartily with them

Anxiety makes you sad

Anxiety breeds these two problems – limitation and fear. A soul battling with these two evils cannot be happy. Anxiety is that culprit that steals your joy by preoccupying you with unnecessary agitation and worry. Happiness is the bedrock of any relationship, so stop being sad and start enjoying happy moments with your partner by taking the following steps:

- Dismiss any thoughts that make you sad.

- Play your favorite music to occupy your mind.

- Become playful with your partner.

- Relive the sweet moments you have had with your partner.

- Be humorous, laugh with your partner.

Anxiety can either make you distant or clingy.

One way by which you can recognize anxious people is that they tend to be extreme in their actions. If they are not aloof, they will become too attached. Both of these behaviors are extreme and unhealthy. Have you evaluated yourself and discovered that you are guilty of these extremities? Take the action steps below to restore your healthy relationship with your partner:

· Figure out your feelings.

· Work on yourself.

· Get yourself engaged with things you enjoy doing.

Anxiety makes you reject things that will benefit you.

It makes you see everything from one point of view - fear. Anxiety results in indecision in a relationship because you won't know which way is right. Here is how you can stop this problem:

· Acknowledge your confusing thoughts and deal with them.

· Weigh your decisions carefully without being biased.

· Seek your partner's help if you discover you need support.

Chapter 5:
Practical Strategies to Solving Anxiety Issues in a Relationship

P artners/couples generally face challenges that need to be addressed as the partnership progresses. Your ability to manage issues as they come up in your relationship will ultimately determine the relationship's growth. If a challenge is not well managed, you may find your relationship in a crisis and may need to take concrete steps towards charting a way out.

Some of the challenges that most people face in their relationships include communication, joint development as a couple, relationship needs, contentedness and autonomy of the partners, equal rights, routine, habit, sexuality, loyalty, stress, quarrels, conflicts, difference in value systems, distance, illness, and the list goes on.

How careful are you in your relationship? Being careful and considerate of each other saves a lot of frustration in the relationship. Do you live in the here and now? Can you enjoy the moment? Living in the here and now sounds easier than it is. More often than not, our thoughts slide into the past or the future.

Other questions to ask yourself about your relationship:

How intensely are you enjoying the moment? Does your partner always understand what you mean? Do you have common interests with your partner? Do you find relish in sharing in each other's lives and experiences? Are both of you a well-rehearsed team in all walks of life? Do you find security, tenderness, and sexual satisfaction with your partner? How about division of labor - does it work well between the both of you? Do you find peace, support, and security in your relationship? Can you talk about everything very openly? Does your partner make you strong and happy?

The answers to these questions will guide you into a proper self-evaluation of the challenges you might be facing in your relationship.

In most cases, men do not like relationship talks. Nevertheless, it is necessary to have regular discussions about needs and wishes in a partnership. Especially for conflict resolution, communication strategies are needed. Firstly, you must distinguish between generally communicating as partners and communication as a result of conflict resolution. Communication about each partner's wishes, ideas, plans, and hopes is an important foundation for a relationship. Couples who are happy in long term relationships are usually able to communicate their feelings to each other. They do not see themselves or their relationship threatened by these expressions, even if they are negative without being aware of it. They can develop their own very subtle language, gestures, and facial expressions throughout their relationship.

Quarrels are normal in a relationship - it is "how they arise" that matters. Clashes arise when you or your partner are strained by external stress. For example, a job, problems in raising children, conflicts in the family, etc. The stressed partner often communicates in a more irritated and violent tone.

It is in our greatest interest to be proactive and inventive regarding how we communicate with those closest to us.

Creating, maintaining, and nurturing relationships with friends, co-workers, and family, not just partners, is critical for our well-being.

Rather than looking to others to create relationship changes, the simplest place to start out is with yourself.

A Relationship Self-Assessment

Below is a list of some relationship statements. Go through the statements and note any that don't seem to apply to you. Write these down on a separate sheet of paper.

1. I have told my spouse/partner/children that I really like them within the previous few days or weeks.

2. I get on well with my siblings.

3. I get on well with my co-workers and/or clients.

4. I get on well with my manager and/or employees.

5. There is nobody I might dread or feel uncomfortable running across.

6. I place relationships first and results second.

7. I have forsaken all of the relationships that drag me down or injury me

8. I have communicated or tried to speak with everybody I may have hurt, injured, or seriously disturbed, though it may not have been 100% my fault.

9. I don't gossip to or about others.

10. I have a circle of friends and/or family who I love and appreciate.

11. I tell people close to me that I appreciate them.

12. I am completely wrapped up in letters, emails, and calls relating to work.

13. I always tell the truth, even if it may hurt.

14. I receive enough love from people around me to feel appreciated.

15. I have forgiven those people that have hurt or broken me, whether or not it was deliberate.

16. I keep my word; people can rely on me.

17. I quickly clear up miscommunications and misunderstandings after they occur.

18. I live life on my terms, not by the principles or preferences of others.

19. There is nothing unresolved with my past lovers or spouses.

20.   I am in tune with my needs and desires and ensure they are taken care of.

21. I don't judge or criticize others.

22.   I have a supporter or lover.

23. I talk openly about issues instead of grumbling.

Chapter 6:
How to Help Your Partner If They Suffer from Relationship Anxiety

Relationships and love demand that we get involved in our partner's life, which means we always have to be supportive and loving. If you have a partner with one or more types of anxiety, you are already aware of how it can influence not just the relationship but also your life. You should know how to recognize the signs and learn how to neutralize an anxiety attack by relying on previous experience.

Your involvement in your partner's journey of learning how to live a life free of anxiety is of great importance. When it comes to sudden panic attacks, you can do several different things to help distract your partner and ease any suffering. When it comes to chronic anxiety, you are the one who will get involved in exposure therapy. There are specific strategies you can take into consideration when it comes to each type of anxiety. This part will help you recognize which kind of stress your partner is struggling with and learn how to help him. You will improve and enhance your relationship's quality, strengthen the bond you have, and confirm your love and devotion to your partner.

Acute Anxiety

Acute anxiety happens out of the blue. It can be caused by different things, specific situations, or other people you and your partner meet. It occurs suddenly, and there is no time for planning and taking it slow. You need to be able to react in the moment and to know how to assess the situation. Understand what is happening, what your partner is going through, and come up with the right way to neutralize the anxiety. There are four ways you can take to be supportive and helpful in case of acute anxiety:

Be calm, be compassionate. If you are not, you won't support your partner's needs in that moment. If you give in to anger, frustration, or anxiety, it won't help. It can even make things worse. You also need to remember not to give in to your partner's anxiety and accommodate it. In the long run, this is not helpful. Instead, offer understanding, not just solutions.

Assess your partner's anxiety. What level is it? What are the symptoms and signs of an anxiety attack? An anxiety attack can hit with a different strength each time. You need to recognize it to choose actions appropriate to the given situation.

Remind your partner of the techniques that helped with previous anxiety attacks. Whether it is breathing or exercise, your partner is probably aware of their success in neutralizing anxiety. But in the given situation, maybe they need reminding. Once they are on the right path to dealing with anxiety, your job is to provide positive reinforcement. Give praise and be empathetic once your partner executes techniques that will help with the attack.

Evaluate the situation. Is your partner's anxiety attack passing? If it is, be supportive and encourage your partner to continue whatever they are doing to lower their anxiety. If it stays at the same level or increases, you should start the steps from the beginning and develop different techniques and strategies to help your partner with an acute anxiety attack.

Chronic Anxiety

To address chronic anxiety, you might have to try out exposure therapy, as it is considered the golden standard of treatment by many people. Usually, it takes the guidance of a professional therapist to try exposure therapy. But, if the level of your partner's anxiety is not severe, you might feel comfortable enough to try it on your own. In this case, you have to guide and learn how to be a supportive person for your partner.

Exposure therapy works by creating situations that trigger your partner's anxiety. It will help your partner learn how to tolerate certain levels of anxiety. Your partner will learn how to reduce anxiety and how to manage it in given situations. Over time, you might get surprised at how your partner now partakes and enjoys situations that previously made them anxious.

You have to start with the least challenging situation and progress slowly and steadily towards more challenging ones. Don't push your partner to the next level until they are ready. If anxiety isn't decreasing in the first challenge, it's not time to go to the second. If a situation is causing too much anxiety, and your partner feels they are not ready to deal with it, go back to the previous challenge, and work on it again.

For example, let's say your partner has a fear of heights. They want to overcome this fear and be able to climb the building's last floor. How will exposure therapy look in this case? Tell your partner to look out the window from the ground floor for precisely one minute.

Climb to the second floor together with your partner. Remember that you are not just an exposure therapy guide; you also need to support them. Make them look out the window from the second floor for one minute. In case of anxiety showing up in its first symptoms, remind your partner to do breathing exercises to reduce its impact.

Once your partner feels better, they should try looking out the window again.

If no anxiety presents itself, you should leave your partner's side. They need to be able to look through the same window, but this time without you.

Climb to the third floor and repeat steps three and four. When your partner feels ready, continue to the fourth floor, sixth, and so on. If your partner's anxiety is too high, don't hesitate to stop. The first session doesn't need to take longer than 30 minutes.

Each new session needs to begin with the last comfortable floor your partner experienced. You don't need to always start from the ground floor, as your partner progresses, feeling no anxiety when looking through the window of the second, third, even fourth floor.

Take time. Your partner will not be free of the fear in just a few days. Be patient and continue practicing exposure therapy in this way until your partner can achieve the goal and climb the last floor.

The goal of exposure therapy is not just to get rid of fear and anxiety. It should also teach your partner that discomfort can be controlled and tolerated. Your partner will have an opportunity to practice anxiety-reduction techniques in a safe and controlled environment, with you playing the supporting role.

Plan for Relieving your Partner's Anxiety

Now you know potential techniques you can use to reduce your partner's anxiety. Use this knowledge to create a plan, make a list of practical actions and ineffective actions when your partner experiences an anxiety attack. It is important to remember what to do in situations that trigger anxiety, but it is also essential to know what not to do.

You and your partner might disagree with what is helpful on the list you are making. It is because your partner craves for accommodative behaviors you express when they are under an anxiety attack. Remember that these behaviors relieve anxiety, but in the long run, they do more damage. Try to explain this to your partner. You need to make them understand why such behavior is not suitable for anyone.

Teamwork is beneficial when it comes to fighting a partner's anxiety. But your partner might not want your help due to feelings of shame or thoughts of not needing help. Try making a list on your own. It's worthwhile to do what you can to elevate your partner's anxiety.

The "What-Works" List

When making a list of things you can do to help your partner with anxiety, it is essential to communicate effectively. Be specific; question your partner how does it make them feel when you perform particular tasks. How does it feel when you join in breathing exercises? Depending on the personality and level of anxiety, they might even want to be left alone. Maybe they need to be reminded during the panic attack to take short breaths and then perform this task alone.

Choose the right intervention for particular symptoms. Learn to recognize your partner's needs in time and offer help.

Here is an example of an anxiety relief list:

- If I am nervously pacing the room and unable to relax, offer to go outside for a walk with me, or suggest taking a walk out alone.

- If I am complaining about work without pause, distract me by choosing a movie we can watch together or suggesting a book I can read alone.

- **If I'm obsessing over whether I turned off the iron, reassure me I did and remind me that not repeatedly checking is one step closer to recovering from my OCD.**

During a panic attack, fast and shallow breathing helps. Remind me how to perform it and join me in this task.

The "What-Doesn't-Work" List

When we love our partner, we feel we will do anything to help him or her. In our efforts to help, we might not realize that we are doing more harm than good. We do mean well, but we don't have the experience, patience, or knowledge of what is happening to our partner during an anxiety attack.

Sometimes even our partner reinforces us to perform tasks that are bad for his anxiety in the long run.

It may look complicated, but both you and your partner need to be honest about behaviors that help alleviate anxiety. It will take time and patience to practice to avoid specific actions that bring relief. Here is an example of a "what-doesn't-work" list:

- I will never again tell my loved one, "just get over it."

- I won't manipulate my partner's feelings to make them stop this behavior.

- I won't use drugs or alcohol to get over my partner's behaviors.

- I won't disrespect my partner's phobias and mock them.

- I won't reinforce my partner's anxiety by accommodating the behavior.

Having a list of what to do and what not to do when anxiety gets triggered will help you and your partner be more in command of your lives. It will stop you from making your partner's anxiety even worse, and it will put both of you on the right track to overcoming the anxiety. Your relationship will become vibrant, more satisfying, and fulfilling. Anxiety cannot be defeated just by taking the steps on the list. They are just things to do to help your partner overcome fear at that point. You will need to take more severe measures to overcome anxiety fully.

A professional therapist will be of great help. It may take some time to find the right therapist for your partner, and it will take some persistence. Therapists may fit one type of personality but not the other. Be sure your partner is paired with the right therapist, and that will help. Encourage and support your partner, and in time you will learn how to manage their anxiety and possibly even watch them completely overcome it.

Chapter 7:
What is jealousy, how to overcome it, what are the symptoms, and how to build trust in the relationship

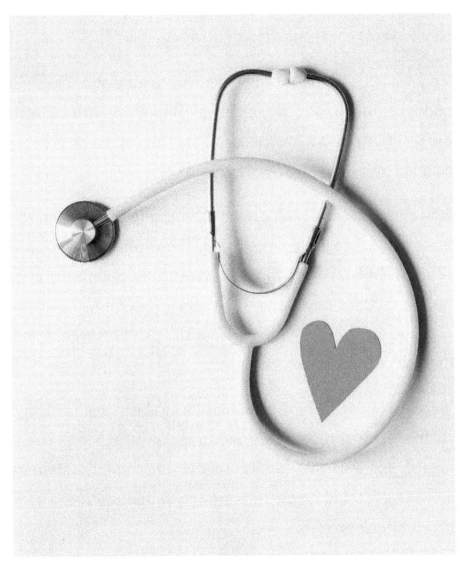

I t is evident to everyone that there is a relationship between love and jealousy, even if this connection is hardly clear: on the one hand, there are those who believe that the jealous lover keeps the couple's intimacy alive and protects it. It is well known that being jealous is often the first step towards the separation of many couples.

Very trivially, jealousy can be defined as an emotional state of doubt and tormenting anxiety of those who, with or without justified reason, fear (or note) that the loved one is being coerced by a rival.

It is a very ancient and ancestral mechanism on which the most famous social convention in the world is based: monogamy. In fact, we choose to stay with the people we love, but the fact of being alone with them is determined by various reasons, which originate from the psycho-social development of the human being.

Since prehistoric times, man has always been jealous of his partner. This is because he had to make sure that he could identify his offspring (and not raise other man's children) and equally could create the certainty of having support for his children's growth.

If initially, this feeling had nothing to do with love, with time and the advent of modern culture, the belief that jealousy and love are somehow connected has grown stronger and stronger, until arriving to affirm that without jealousy, there is no love.

But is it true that you cannot love if you are not jealous? And if so, how much and how should we be jealous?

"Healthy" Jealousy

It could be said that jealousy is the fear of losing what we care about, and, in the case of relationships, this concept is identified with the fear that the loved one stops wanting us and prefers anyone else to us.

If we want to prevent this person from leaving our life, we should not be indifferent to signs (real or alleged) that they begin to snub our attention or ignore us to devote their time to others.

At this point, the issue of limits arises.

Above what level is jealousy "acceptable" and useful for properly preserving a relationship, and when does it become harmful and destructive?

It could be said that this depends on the role we play in the relationship and on how the subject that threatens us (real or imaginary) tries to insinuate itself into this relational space.

For example, suppose a man sees another man courting his wife. In that case, it is right and healthy for the relationship that this situation generates a certain level of jealousy in him, precisely because his role in the exclusive relationship with his partner is threatened.

Every lasting relationship contains many feelings, experiences, and a wealth of mutual knowledge that the two partners must dutifully defend to not lose their identity as a couple.

This is why a suitor, or worse, a lover, can tear a relationship to pieces even before they have succeeded in their intent: ousting the partner from their role is often enough to undermine the balance of the couple.

Romantic Jealousy

Jealousy of someone you love and fear losing is called romantic jealousy in literature. The dynamic of romantic jealousy develops in a triangle made up of three fundamental elements: 'The Self' (the jealous person), 'the Loved One,' and 'the Rival.'

The dynamics of amorous jealousy and its constituents:

1.   The belief that some relationships are configured as objects of possession and give the right to request or prohibit certain behaviors (even to prohibit, paradoxically, feelings and desires);

2.   The fear that 'the Rival' will or may undermine the possession and enjoyment of 'the Loved One,' causing partial or complete loss;

3.   The prediction that if this were to happen, the jealous person would have damage (suffering from the loss of the object of love or its exclusivity) and a bruised self-esteem.

This type of jealousy is characterized by a strong feeling of possessiveness towards the loved one and, therefore, by believing that you have the right to prohibit or impose certain behaviors on your partner. However, sometimes one can also be jealous of almost unknown people, which excludes the absolute presence in the dynamic of jealousy of possessiveness. In relationships, there is sometimes the fear of losing the loved one because of the rival. This fear is present even if, in reality, the real threat of a third wheel in the couple relationship is completely absent.

Another important element in this type of jealousy would be the expectation of possible harm if the loved one were to betray; that damage would lead to a strong loss of self-esteem. Therefore, it is easy to understand how situations that cause jealousy can have real foundations but can also be caused by unfounded fears projected by the jealous person within the relationship or by minor behaviors that simply overshadow the risk or suspicion of infidelity. As for 'the Rival,' some authors point out that the most feared rival is the one who possesses the positive characteristics that approach one's ideal self, rather than the ideal of the loved one.

Is Hunger for Love, Anxiety, and Depression Related?

Love, with its sweet seductions, false truths, and atrocious acts of revenge, has been walking alongside us since we were children, and thanks to it, we are born, we grow up, we feed ourselves, and, sometimes, we poison ourselves.

Is love, hunger for love, anxiety, and mood deflection inter-related?

Apparently disjoint, they seem three elements without any connection between them, but in reality, they are closely connected and intersected with each other.

We know well that the ability to choose a partner first and being a couple afterward depends on how we have been loved and, more importantly if we have been loved.

Childhood, Autonomy, Dependence, and Love

The early experiences of care nourish the soul and self-esteem and then contribute to transforming that child, in need of care and love, into an independent adult, serene and capable of relating to their partner and the world, without that child's atavistic wound often carried around if they are "not loved."

The "wound of the unloved" is often the cause of a lack of basic trust and love if it affects our partners and the bond of love.

The partner is not chosen only based on physical and personal attraction, but on the basis of a lot of other things, often "invisible to the eye."

Many love stories are stories between accomplices and childhoods - or childhood chasms - alike.

The choices of love are often "collusive choices." Many times the chosen partners are those who, in some way, lead back to the land of childhood.

The hunger for love, closely related to the "wound of the unloved" - that atavistic lack of love, like an indelible mark, moves the ranks of affective and relational choices - are closely related to anxiety and the deflection of the tone of the mood.

Couples, Love, and Separation Anxiety

Working steadily with couples, shipwrecked, unresolved, separating or separated, I can say that the health of the couple and their quality of life depends on the health of each protagonist of that bond, from how and if they were loved, and from the ability they have to give within the bond of love.

- Anxiety by separation

Another element of central importance is separation anxiety.

When one of the two, or both the protagonists of that love, is moved by crazy jealousy, by an impetuous need to control the other, and by the fear - almost terror - of losing the partner, there are all the elements to shipwreck - sooner or later - that bond.

It is, in fact, a "hungry, needy, dependent love," a bond in which victim and executioner alternate, nourishing and keeping alive the emotional dependence.

In 'Fragments of a Love Discourse,' Roland Barthes wrote in a very suggestive way: "I hurt the other."

Some Symptoms of the Hunger for Love

The hunger for love almost always manifests itself with the same characteristics, atrocious and unbearable:

- An unbridgeable need for love

- A sadness dreadful to bear

- Love seen and experienced as an aid

- Hyper investment by the partner

- A despairing dedication to the beloved

- Savage jealousy

- Possessiveness

- Need for confirmation and certainty

- Anxiety and separation anxiety

- Never feeling loved enough

- Lack of interest in oneself and one's own interests (with an emotional shift towards the partner)

- Extreme devotion

- Anxiety and panic in the face of any mishap or temporary distance from the partner

- The total absence of borders with the partner, tendency toward symbiosis, and a fusional relationship

The protagonists of these sick loves are often unresolved on the psychic level and are trying to find the cure for the soul's ailments in love and a relationship.

So, can anxiety and depression be the cause and consequence of the hunger for love?

In those suffering from addiction, love becomes a drug, a real psycho/physical necessity, to the point of transforming itself into the joy and pain of their own life.

They are crazy loves.

Unhealthy Love

Love, inhabited by excesses, imbalances, lack of balance.

These loves are loves characterized by a massive desire, never completely satisfied, of absolute and fusional love - always and in any case nourished by abandonment anxieties - often moved by the need for confirmation from the other.

Symptoms of Anxiety and Mood Deflection

When love brings suffering with it, sooner or later, the body begins to complain, to cry out that something is wrong, and that love will tend to be wrecked.

The body, as we know, expresses itself with the language of symptoms which, in reality, are the gateway to the soul:

- Various aches and pains, sine causa

- Psycho-motor agitation

- Endless sleepless nights counting sheep

- Disorders of the oral-alimentary sphere

- Tachycardia.

- Palpitations, the strange and annoying sensation of feeling the heart

- Pain in the center of the chest

- Pressure drops

- The terrifying feeling of having lost control over one's body, and one's destiny

- Breathing difficulties and a feeling of suffocation

- Increased urinary frequency

- Disorders of the menstrual cycle

- Sexual response disorders: anorgasmia and sexual desire disorders

- Diffuse and somatic anxiety

- Irritability, inability to unplug

- Ease of crying, poor modulation of emotions

In summary, our body is the litmus test of our soul and our psycho / physical well-being or malaise.

Listening to it, taking care of it, and having the ability to understand if a Love is a love that nourishes or impoverishes, cares for, or destabilizes, is the quickest way to happiness, or at least, serenity.

Chapter 8:
How to eliminate negative thinking and the fear of abandonment

I n addressing negative thoughts, various approaches can help. The good news is that this manual will shed light on the best ways to deal with your ideas to prevent it from graduating to anxiety disorder.

One meaningful and helpful way is to make mental shifts. In other words, intentionally adjusting the way you think of challenging an established thought pattern. This happens by changing the way you judge an event or situation. It is a form of training for the brain such that it doesn't succumb to anxiety generating thoughts.

This will not be a straightforward process because it involves "uninstalling" and "deprogramming" many negative behaviors and thinking patterns responsible for anxiety. For instance, if, as a little girl, your dad kept hammering that no one will love you if you are fat, you end up being haunted by that for life. Hence, you might even resort to unhelpful means to try and keep fit.

Beware of thoughts that place excessive demands on you. They start with "I" or "should." Many a time, these demands are impossible to live up to, which ends up fueling our anxiety. Consider the following:

Instead of...	Try...
I should wake up early tomorrow.	I will sleep early and try to wake up early tomorrow.
I should stop eating this kind of food.	These food items are not healthy for me. I need to be in good health; hence taking... will help.
I should make more friends.	I need to go out more often, make myself approachable, and smile, hoping someone will notice and talk to me.

The problem with this sort of thought is the compulsion and pressure it puts on us. When this gets to an unbearable level, we end up procrastinating or avoiding what we want to do as a means of escaping. In the long run, this ends up triggering more anxiety.

With this in mind, rather than telling yourself you should do things, think of a kind, calm and gentle approach to keep yourself motivated towards the task before you. You can think of another means without graduating into a negative thought pattern.

How to Control Negative Thoughts to Beat Anxiety.

The good news is that you can take many positive steps to have a turnaround and break free of the cycle of thoughts that causes anxiety. You can come up with a viable strategy to counter those thoughts to prevent anxiety. This section explores how you can control negative thoughts:

Turn Negative to Positive Action

Should you be bewildered by an obsessive thought that's calling you to do something, listen to the dictate of that thought and attend to it. In the same way, you will not ignore the check engine light of your vehicle forever. No matter how hard you try to avoid looking at it, it is right before you every time you are driving. You will not, because of the check engine light, discard the vehicle or give it out. In the same manner, should thought be a cry for help, do not ignore it.

In other words, take a break and attend to the situation. If you feel scared and tense to the extent of triggering anxiety, take a break and consider what is making you afraid. Rather than pushing the feeling away, take some time off, examine why you are scared, and look for how to address it.

Once you are calm enough to deal with the matter, come up with an action plan. By this, I mean positive and actionable steps that can help. Doing this should address the real source of the anxiety rather than push the thoughts away.

Avoid Indulging in the Level of Futility

In dealing with unhelpful thoughts, there is a tendency to keep doing what doesn't work. However, the problem is evident – they never work. The issue is how easy it is easy for the brain to succumb to these useless tactics repeatedly.

With this in mind, rather than falling back to self-defeating thoughts, consider another approach. It is not about fighting old habits but noticing what doesn't work and sticking to what does.

Expand Your Awareness

A constricted mind is like a tight muscle. The degree of movement will be minimal. A few of the things that constrict the mind are old beliefs, inertia, habits, fear, low expectations, and old conditioning. You, however, need to confront this with all honesty.

A closed mindset does no good. With this in mind, on detecting any inner discomfort, be sure to expand your awareness. For instance, a feeling of hatred towards your neighbor is a clear example of a contracted mindset. However, with an open mindset, you can tolerate the person and see another good side of them rather than seek out their fault.

Combat Shades of Green Thinking

Our mind has been conditioned to taking the easy way out. In thinking and making decisions, we love the easy way as it speeds our progress and helps our decision making. This is about dealing with black and white thinking patterns, which could be challenging as it holds the person to irrational beliefs.

Rather than getting anxious with shades of gray thought, I recommend evaluating circumstances on a scale of 0 to 10. Falling short of expectations should be seen as a partial failure, rather than sinking into anxiety and beating yourself up.

For instance, someone could say, "I am very useless; I could not wake up to go over my notes for this evening's exam." However, how sure are you that missing a single morning will affect your chance of success? When you analyze this on a scale, it could be a 7% likelihood. This helps removes the anxiety of looking at the circumstance in terms of complete failure.

See Disappointments as Part of Life

You might not be able to do much about disappointments. With this in mind, condition your mind to expect them once in a while. Avoid overthinking people and circumstances so that when things go in a way you didn't anticipate, the blow will not be too much. Life will throw a lot at you. Bear in mind that your reactions to all the happenings have a lot to do with your well-being. You can either sink into anxiety or rise above it, seeing it as part of life.

It is vital to know the difference between the things you can control and the ones you cannot. It takes a wise man to let go of things he cannot control. This is the secret to happiness and rising above anxiety that comes with disappointments. You were jilted despite your faithfulness and dedication to the relationship. It hurts, I know, but mourn it and move forward, preparing yourself for the next available partner.

Challenging Unhelpful Thoughts

Our thoughts and the way we give in to thinking can affect our anxiety levels. Most of these thoughts take place outside our control and are often hostile and irrelevant. We should always remember that these are mere thoughts; they have no solid basis and are not always facts.

Although it is straightforward to believe most of our irrelevant thoughts when we are anxious, we should also remember that they are often wrong assumptions, most times figments of our imaginations, and need to be questioned.

Fear of Abandonment

Fear of abandonment is the overriding fear that people will leave near you.

Everyone can develop a fear of giving up. It can be deeply rooted in your traumatic experience as a child or in adult depression.

When you fear failure, maintaining healthy relationships can be almost impossible. The paralyzing fear will drive you away to avoid being harmed. Or you may be sabotaging partnerships unintentionally.

The first step to overcoming anxiety is to understand why you feel like that. You can address your fears on your own or through therapy. However, fear of abandonment may also be part of a personality disorder requiring treatment.

Different Types of Fear of Abandonment

You may fear that someone you love will physically leave and not come back. You might be afraid someone will give up your emotional needs. You can either maintain yourself in ties with a parent, partner, or friend. Examples of abandonment fear:

Fear of Emotional Abandonment

It may be less noticeable, but it is no less painful.

Emotional needs exist for us all. In case these conditions are not met, you may feel unrecognized, unloved, and disconnected. You may feel very much alone, even if you are in a relationship with a physically present person.

If you have undergone emotional renunciation in the past, especially as a child, you may always be afraid that it will happen again.

Fear of Abandonment in Children

It is normal for babies and children to experience a period of separation fear.

They may scream, yell or refuse to let go if a parent or caregiver is leaving. At this stage, children have difficulty understanding when or if the person will return.

As they begin to understand that they come back, they resolve their terror. This happens to most children by their 3rd birthday.

Abandonment Anxiety In relationships

You can actually be afraid of allowing yourself to be insecure in a relationship. You may have problems of confidence and worry about your relationship too much. That can make your partner suspicious.

Over time, the anxieties will cause the other person to retreat and keep the cycle going.

Symptoms of The Fears of Abandonment

When you fear abandonment, you can likely identify some of these symptoms and signs:

- Too sensitive to criticism

- Trouble trusting in others

- Difficulty making friends unless you are sure you want them

- Take extreme measures to prevent rejections or separation

- Pattern of unhealthy relationships

- Staying in a relationship even at the point that it is not healthy for you

- Blaming yourself when things don't work

- Trouble committing into a relationship

- Working too hard to please people

- Getting attached to people quickly and moving on quickly

Causes of Abandonment

Abandonment problems in relationships may be due to having been emotionally or physically abandoned in the past.

For example:

• As an infant, a parent or caregiver may have died or just up and left.

• Parental negligence may have been felt.

• Your colleagues might have rejected you.

• You have been through a loved one's chronic illness.

• A romantic partner may have suddenly left you or acted untruthfully.

These events can lead to a fear of abandonment.

Long-Term Effects of Fear of Abandonment

The long-term effects of the fear of giving up may include:

• Challenging connections with friends and romantic partners

• Poor self-esteem

- Issues with self-confidence

- Mood swings

- Codependence

- Depression

- Fear of intimacy

- Panic problems

Examples of the Fear of abandonment

Here are a few examples of what the fear of giving up may look like:

Longer-term effects of fear of abandonment, you may think, "No connection, no drop."

- You are obsessively worried about your perceived flaws and what others might think about you.

- You are the most pleasant people. You don't want to take any opportunity that someone doesn't like you to stay there.

- You are crushed when someone criticizes you a little or gets upset in any way.

- When you feel slighted, you overreact

- You feel insufficient and unattractive.

- You split with a romantic partner so that they can't break up with you.

- Even if the other person asks for space, you are clingy.

- You are often jealous, suspicious of your partner, or critical of him.

Fear of abandonment is not a diagnosed mental health disorder, but it can be detected and discussed. Fear of rejection may also be part of a diagnosable personality or another condition to be treated.

Recovery Problems

Once you know that you fear loss, you can do some things to start recovery.

Remove some slackness and stop the harsh judgment on yourself. Mind all the positive qualities that make you the right partner and mate.

Speak to the other person about how this fear came to be. But be aware of what you deserve from others. Explain where you come from, but don't make up something to fix your fear of abandonment. Don't expect more than is fair from them.

Work to maintain friendships and build a support network. Strong friendships will strengthen your sense of belonging and self-worth.

If this is not practical, consider talking to a qualified therapist. You will benefit from individual advice.

How to Assist Someone with Abandonment Problems

Some strategies you can try if someone you know has to deal with the fear of abandonment:

• Begin the conversation. Encourage them to speak, but don't press.

• Understand that the fear is real for them, whether it makes sense or not.

• Make sure you're not going to abandon them.

• Ask what you can do to assist.

• Suggest treatment but don't push it. If you want to start, offer your help in finding a professional therapist.

See your healthcare provider for guidance if you have attempted but cannot manage your fear of self-abandonment or if you have signs of panic disorder, anxiety disorder, or depression.

You should continue a full check-up with your primary care physician. You can then consult a doctor to diagnose and treat the illness.

Personality disorders can lead to depression, substance use, and social isolation without treatment.

Fear of abandonment will affect your relationships negatively. But you can do things to minimize these fears.

If the fear of dropping out is part of a broader personality disorder, drugs and psychotherapy can successfully treat it.

Chapter 9:
How to resolve conflicts and save your relationship (especially in marriage)

I t's quick to miss one aspect in today's world of television dating shows, mobile applications, and romantic comedies: relationships are work. They need time and commitment. We never "swipe correctly," fall in love, and live happily ever after. And when things get rough, it's easy to throw in the towel, suggest, "it wouldn't have worked out anyway," and step on – rather than do the work to learn how to maintain a relationship.

But it's worth protecting your relationship.

You've got a past. You've been through a lot together – a lot of relationships over the last few years or even decades before you came to this stage. Your partner loves you better than anybody else, so they're going to be there for you when no one else would. Before you give up all hope, seek these nine ideas about how to save your relationship.

1. *Examine your focus*

Conflict is dangerous as you concentrate on protecting yourself against assault rather than on solving the issue. It's because people's minds will be focused on avoiding "hitting the pole," in other words, not confronting problems because they believe they have an out-clause. But our attention is on our course. If we don't want to hit the pole, we need to focus on what we want to do: stay on the road! We may change the result by shifting our emphasis.

This lesson is on how to save your relationship. When you focus on where you don't want the relationship to stop, struggle, and allow frustration to build-up, you'll find yourself where you don't want to be — either in a miserable, unfulfilling relationship or totally apart from the spouse. If you work on dispute management and evolve together, you'll get the results you expect.

2. *Communicate*

Two couples were faced with a dispute – the same problem, in reality. But one of them understood how to settle a dispute in a relationship, and the other did not. One responded by depending on bad behaviors and using the disagreement to enlarge the distance between them. The other used confrontation as a way to express their emotions and grow their relationship. What couple do you think has the most positive, satisfying relationship? What kind of relationship do you think would last longer? Communication is at the top of the list of ways to preserve a relationship.

3. Turn conflict into opportunity

Don't get defensive; don't pound your point; don't attempt to fight: one couple has learned these ways to settle a dispute in their relationship. Do you still want to sacrifice your partner, the one you love? If you agree that there are no losers in life, you will let go of small disagreements and indulge in good conversation.

Conflicts are ways for you and your partner to match beliefs and consequences. They are likely to recognize, respect, and accept disparities. Put yourself in your partner's position and seek to grasp his or her understanding. Such experiences and emotions may be painful, but we will never develop if we only want comfort.

Conflict is also a way to know more about your partner and to respect them more intensely. Begin to see disagreement as a step to something new, rather than as a cause to withdraw. The next time you find yourself disagreeing with your spouse and contemplating how to save your relationship, remember to see the best in the scenario rather than the bad, and consciously trying to work together towards a more stable future.

4. Use humor

If you're in a retaliatory loop, a strong strategy is to use comedy to interrupt the trend. Humor will relieve stress and enable you and your partner to concentrate on what you really want – discovering how to sustain the relationship – rather than on what you just don't want, another meaningless fight. If you notice the argument is worsening, take a minute to stop it. Try talking to Christopher Walken or William Shatner. Singing a song that makes your partner laugh. Render the tension too absurd.

Few spouses would have transformed the scenario into a dispute, but by using comedy to nip the cycle of retribution in the bud, you and your partner can seize the moment and converted it into an opportunity to practice how to resolve the conflict in the relationship.

5. Ask the right questions

If you're considering how to save a relationship, it's possible that things have been going bad for quite some time. Not only do you need to reach into the background to discover the specific, deeper problems, but you need to look to the future. It's just about asking the correct questions about yourself.

Second, make sure you continue this exercise with the best mind. The point is not to criticize, dig up old arguments, or remind your partner of all the stuff they're doing that annoys you. You will shift your attitude to one of appreciation and approval. Take note of the reality that life is going on for your partner, not just for you. Even your relationship's present condition offers you an opportunity to improve and develop – as long as you remain responsive to what it has to teach you.

Now you're brave enough to ask yourself the most critical questions: Why did your relationship break down? Are these the restricting values that have influenced the relationship between you and the partner? How are you going to conquer them? What do you like about the future? What's the relationship going to depend on?

6. *Practice acceptance*

Apply your new open-mindedness to your partner. Our partners do somethings or have behaviors that annoy us because no human being is perfect. Instead of focusing on their derogatory attributes or poor behavior, concentrate on what they bring to the table, how they make you look, and the things you enjoy. You will notice that you will quickly begin to enjoy all the things that used to make you mad, as they are part of the whole person, your partner, whom you love.

Respond to your partner, consider what they think and why they act the way they do it. And understand yourself, too: be frank with your own thoughts and emotions. Be thy own self. Human shortcomings aren't meant to be the explanation of why you're wondering how to save your relationship. Basically, they're a great tool to show your partner how much you value them.

7. *Be aware of your negative patterns*

Conflict with your spouse can make you feel assaulted or endangered, helpless and fragile, which may make you panic and retreat. When something that your spouse does annoy you, and you feel like you're under attack, you're less inclined to react constructively, so you're more apt to return to old standbys like "the silent treatment" that can eventually do more damage than good. Eventually, that would lead the relationship to break down entirely.

If anyone asked you if you know how to settle a dispute, you would undoubtedly say yes, and if they asked you if passive treatment was a good approach to cope with the issue, you would almost definitely answer no. You know better than to succumb to these dumb tactics, but if you're upset enough, you do it anyway. Why? Why? Why fall back on destructive habits instead of actively trying to correct the relationship problems at hand?

Break the cycle of aggression and offer constructive energies to the dispute. Don't take the defensive; don't pound the point; don't try to defend. How would you want to sacrifice your partner, the one you love?

8. Work on forgiveness

When you're considering how to save your relationship when your confidence has fallen, you're likely to feel furious, frustrated, wounded, and mistrustful, and a variety of other negative emotions. When you're the one who broke the trust, you feel bad and ashamed. You may also seek to condemn your partner or defend your acts. All spouses need to focus on reconciliation in this case.

You're not only going to wake up every day and feel good about forgiving your partner. Forgiveness is a form of process. It's a collection of little actions – admitting faults, exercising total integrity, and placing your partner first – that adds up over time. Forgiveness is taking a role.

If you broke your partner's trust, you would have to take complete responsibility. Be mindful of how badly you upset your partner, and give them the support they deserve. Place the partner first so you don't slip into a trap of self-denial. If your faith is lost, take some space, but keep communicating. Let your spouse realize what you need to restore your trust. Most of all, never give up on that.

9. Make time for touch

When you're always fighting with your partner — when every little thing they do bothers you — it can be hard to be affectionate. But you've got to make time for touch. It doesn't only mean sex – it also means cuddling on the sofa during a movie, stealing a morning kiss before work, and holding hands for no reason at all.

There's a reason why loving your partner helps you feel so good: cuddling, kissing, and even rubbing your hands, triggers the production of oxytocin, a "feel-good" hormone in your brain lets you feel protected and secure. Oxytocin will reduce pain, help you relax, make you feel more connected to your partner, and also reduce your blood pressure. You get all the advantages of getting over and taking your partner's hand.

Don't deny physical affection – except when you're upset – otherwise, you may find yourself in a totally sexless relationship or marriage. If you really want to learn how to save your relationship, continue with your physical contact. Cuddling until bedtime. Keep your hands while you're out for dinner with your friends. Sneak in a hug when you're enjoying dinner. Physical affection is not the product of a good relationship – it produces a happier relationship. Relationships aren't that simple. We are all people, and human beings make mistakes. We've got weaknesses. Sometimes, we just don't get into the work that we need to do, and we just let our relationships fall by the wayside. When we start looking at ways to save a relationship, it may have been ignored for years. But note this: a lot of relationships are worth preserving. You also need to be able to do some sort of work.

Conclusion

I t is important to take care of yourself while in a relation-ship because you are not only responsible for your own well-being but the well-being of your partner. Remember that there are resources out there just waiting to help you get through this tough time. It is a process, but there are ways to get better. Everything will be okay!

Love is enjoyable when you let go of the anxiety that comes between you and your partner. When you give anxiety a chance to run free in your love life, it may be difficult to know when and how to react to sensitive situations. This may lead you to feel indifferent or unconcerned to some vital relation-ship issues or put on a show of being uninvolved and forceful when speaking with your partner. While it's certainly not your fault, it's beneficial to understand how anxiety may be affecting how you see things.

When it feels like anxiety is genuinely keeping you down, you will need to overcome it both for your well-being and your relationship's health. By putting all the tips and techniques learned from this book into action, you will be able to over-come every anxiety and insecurity in your relationship. The strategies in this book aim to help you learn positive adapt-ing attitudes to managing your anxiety in the right manner. That can mean having a more advantageous relationship by maintaining a strategic distance from certain anxiety-related errors.

Anxiety is love's most noteworthy executioner. It makes others feel as if you are suffocating them. It's not easy to overcome this, but it's possible.

Anxiety makes it hard to realize what's important and what's not. It can blow things out of proportion, distract us, and cripple us. But it doesn't have to control us.

You deserve to be in a happy, loving relationship that isn't marred by anxiety's vicious grip. All it takes is a conscious effort and a new perspective to realize that anxiety's weakness is a loving connection. By strengthening your relationship, you weaken anxiety's grasp. What's a better example of a win-win than that?

CPSIA information can be obtained
at www.ICGtesting.com
Printed in the USA
BVHW040809010321
601200BV00016B/220